CONTENTS

TOP FOOTBALL

British football is popular all over the planet! Millions of people watch it on TV.

THE FOOTBALL LEAGUE

The Football League has 92 teams from England and Wales. There are four divisions.

The top division is the Premiership. Over 200 different countries show Premiership matches on TV.

Old Trafford is the biggest club stadium in the UK. Over 75,000 people can watch matches there.

SPORT

UK

Peters
Publishing

Author: Moira Butterfield

First published in 2016 by Peters Publishing

120 Bromsgrove Street
Birmingham
West Midlands
B5 6RJ

ISBN: 978-0-9935457-1-9
Dewey number: 796.04

Commissioned, designed,
edited and project managed
for Peters Publishing by Dynamo LImited.

Author: Moira Butterfield
Educational consultant: Gill Matthews

Alamy: Roger Cracknell 01/classic p27(t).

Corbis: David Kissman/ActionPlus/Corbis p5(t), Vagelis Georgariou/ActionPlus/ Corbis p5(b), touchlinepics Steve Gaunt/Demotix/Corbis p7(t), Andrew Surma/ Demotix/Corbis p7(b), Visionhaus/Corbis p9(b), Splash News/Splash News/ Corbis p10(b), Splash News/Splash News/Corbis p11(t), OLIVIA HARRIS/Reuters/ Corbis p13(t), Martin Avery/Demotix/Corbis p13(m), Chris Young/Demotix/Corbis p13(b), Homer Sykes/Corbis p14(b), TimClayton/Corbis p15(t), Tim Clayton/Corbis p15(m), Vova Pomortzeff/Demotix/Corbis p15(b),Chris Strickland/Demotix/ Corbis p17(t), Relay Images/Demotix/Corbis p17(m),Mark Kerton/ActionPlus/ Corbis p17(b),Marc Casolani/Demotix/Corbis p20(b), Carlo Borlenghi/NewSport/ Corbis p21(b), Steve Bardens/Corbis p22(b), POOL/Reuters/Corbis p23(t), Denis Balibouse/Reuters/Corbis p23(ml), Markus Scholz/dpa/Corbis p23(mr), Philippe Turpin/Photononstop/Corbis p29(t).

Getty: Ian MacNicol/Contributor p24(b), Alexander Hassenstein/Staff p25(t), TOSHIFUMI KITAMURA/Staff p25(m), OLI SCARFF/Stringer p27(b), Handout/ Handout p28(b).

Rex: Mark Bullimore/REX Shutterstock p26(b).

Shutterstock: naipung p4(m), iconsprop4(t), Victor Soares p5(t), kuroksta p6(t), Vitezslav Valka p6(m), Victor Soares p6(b), PinkPueblo p8(t), Mitch Gunn p8(m), SurangaSL p8(t), SurangaSL p9(t), IG_Studio p10(tr), pukach p10(tm), Stuart Slavicky p11(b), doomu p12(t), Michaelpuche p12(m), Bikeworldtravel p12(b), Vaclav Volrab p14(t), Natykach Nataliia p16(t), Vitezslav Valka p16(m), Grzegorz Petrykowski p16(b), BAKOUNINE p18(b), BAKOUNINE p19(t), MrSegui p19(m), AHMAD FAIZAL YAHYA p19(b), Alvov p20(m), tassel78 p20(t), PHB.cz (Richard Semik) p21(t), Africa Studio p22(t), Stefan Holm p22(m), Nordling p24(t), Yoko Design p24(m), Olga Besnard p25(b), MARKBZ p26(t), Germanskydiver p29(b).

Cover Images: Corbis Tim Clayton/Corbis (bl), Corbis Denis Balibouse/ Reuters/Corbis) (tl), Corbis Chris Strickland/Demotix/Corbis (tr), Shutterstock Germanskydiver (br), Shutterstock iconsprop4 (mr), Shutterstock IG_Studio (t), Shutterstock MARKBZ (tr), Shutterstock Nordling (mr), Getty OLI SCARFF / Stringer (b).

Printed in the United Kingdom

Peters Publishing is an imprint of Peters Books and Furniture
120 Bromsgrove Street
Birmingham
West Midlands
B5 6RJ

www.peters-books.co.uk

THE FA CUP

There are FA Cup competitions for men's teams and women's teams. The men's FA Cup began over 140 years ago. It is the oldest football competition in the world.

The finals are played at Wembley — England's national stadium.

OLDEST TROPHY

Scotland has its own League. Men's and women's teams also compete for the Scottish Cup. The men's silver trophy is the oldest national trophy in the world.

The men's Scottish Cup trophy is worth £2 million.

TOP RUGBY

Over two million people play Rugby Union or Rugby League in the UK. The two sports have different rules.

SHOWDOWN FOR SIX

ENGLAND   ITALY

SCOTLAND   WALES

IRELAND   FRANCE

Every year, six countries battle it out for the Rugby Union Six Nations Championship.

If a team wins all its matches, it is called a Grand Slam winner. The team that comes last gets 'the wooden spoon'. There isn't a real spoon — the idea of it is bad enough!

England, Wales, Scotland, Ireland, France and Italy are the big six.

LEAGUE WINNERS

Rugby League teams compete in a British league for the Challenge Cup. Wigan have won the cup the most times.

Teams from France and Russia take part in the Challenge Cup, too. Here a French team, Catalan Dragons, play Leeds Rhinos.

There are 15 people in a Rugby Union team. There are 13 people in a Rugby League team.

CRAZY ABOUT CRICKET

People have played cricket in the UK for at least 400 years. Nearly one million people still play it.

TOP TEAMS

The top teams in the UK are called county teams. In summer, they play each other in the County Championship, and in cup competitions too.

The England team plays test matches against teams from other countries, such as Australia, India and Pakistan.

Joe Root batting for England in a test match against Australia in 2015.

Lord's cricket ground in London is called the 'home of cricket'. It has a museum of cricket treasures.

THE ASHES URN

The England team plays Australia over five matches for the Ashes. The winner gets a tiny trophy — the Ashes urn.

The urn is over 130 years old. It was made in 1882, when Australia beat England for the first time on English soil. It was a joke to represent the death of English cricket!

TOP TENNIS

Wimbledon is the world's oldest tennis championship. Every summer more than 600 players from all over the world take part.

A HUNDRED YEARS OF GRASS

Wimbledon first began over 130 years ago. Just 22 players were in the very first contest.

Andy Murray won the men's singles title at Wimbledon in 2013. He was the first British man to win since 1936!

WORLD'S RICHEST

Wimbledon gives out more prize money than any other tennis contest. The winners of the singles titles take home £1.88 million.

In 2015, US tennis star Serena Williams won the women's singles title at Wimbledon. She also won the US, Australian and French titles!

BRILLIANT BALLS

Over 50,000 tennis balls are used at Wimbledon every year. Each one is tested to make sure it bounces perfectly.

200 ball boys and ball girls are trained to help the Wimbledon players during matches.

MARATHON MAGIC

Britain hosts some great marathons and half-marathons. Thousands of runners compete, from ordinary people to world champion athletes.

LONDON RUNNING

Around 38,000 people take part in the London Marathon in spring every year. They run for 42.2 kilometres across the city.

Many of the runners are sponsored to raise money for charity. In 2015, the London Marathon raised over £54 million.

WHEELCHAIR WHIZZ

The London Wheelchair Marathon is on the same day. Contestants use racing wheelchairs and can go up to 30 kilometres per hour.

Britain's David Weir has won the London Wheelchair Marathon many times.

IT'S GREAT UP NORTH!

The Great North Run is the biggest half-marathon in the world. Around 54,000 people do it every September.

British champion Mo Farah won the Great North Run in 2015.

SADDLE STARS

The world's best riders and horses take part in British eventing and horse racing.

BEST OF THREE

Horses and riders compete in three events over three days. It's called 'three-day-eventing'.

Dressage

Horses and riders perform a set of complex moves.

Show jumping

Horses and riders must jump over fences without knocking them down.

Cross country

Horses and riders compete over a long course, jumping fences and ditches.

The Badminton and the Burleigh Horse Trials are Britain's top eventing competitions.

PROUD CROWD

Around six million people go to see horse-racing events in Britain each year. Only football draws bigger crowds.

There are two kinds of horse racing — flat racing and jump racing. It is called flat racing because the horses don't jump over fences.

Jump racing is also called steeplechasing. Some jumps have ditches of water on the other side.

STAR CYCLING

Over two million people cycle every week in the UK. No wonder we have world-beating cycling champions!

TOUR OF BRITAIN

The Tour of Britain is the biggest cycling road race in the country. Over a million people go to see it.

The Tour is Britain's biggest free sporting event.

WINNING OFF-ROAD

Mountain bikers have a National Championship. The winner wears a jersey with rainbow stripes.

The Mountain Biking Championship is held on a muddy, hilly track, with logs, rocks and streams to ride over.

TRACK ATTACK

Cyclists race round the sloped walls of the velodrome track at speeds up to 80 kilometres per hour. There are many different races, from one-on-one contests to team events.

Britain's Sir Chris Hoy won six Olympic gold medals and 11 World Championships on the track.

British cyclist Lizzie Armitstead is a World Champion on both the track and road.

MOTOR MAGIC

Every year, the planet's fastest racing drivers and motorbike stars race around the track at Silverstone.

ON TRACK

Formula 1 racing drivers compete in the British Grand Prix. They race 52 laps at up to 328 kilometres per hour.

The cars take the fastest corner at Silverstone at 302 kilometres per hour!

A Formula 1 Car can be worth up to £6 million.

CHAMPION OF CHAMPIONS

Lewis Hamilton has won the British Grand Prix more than once, as well as the Formula One World Championship.

Lewis Hamilton began racing in go-karts. He won his first kart championship when he was eight years old.

MotoGP Grand Prix bikes are worth around £1 million each.

BRILLIANT BIKES

At the British MotoGP, motorbike stars such as Valentino Rossi roar round the Silverstone track. They race for 20 laps at speeds over 177 kilometres per hour.

SEA STARS

Every two years the world's top sailors compete in the Fastnet Race. It is one of the world's hardest yacht races.

ACROSS TO IRELAND

The Fastnet race starts at Cowes on the Isle of Wight. The boats race around the coast, then over to Ireland and back.

About 350 boats take part. The race is difficult and dangerous when the weather gets windy and the sea is rough.

Only the best sailors and top yachts are allowed to race.

The sailors must avoid dangers such as the Fastnet Rock off the coast of Ireland.

These boats are starting the Fastnet Race. The record for completing the race is 44 hours and 18 minutes.

WINNING IN WATER

Swimming is the most popular sport in the UK. Around three million people go swimming every week.

POOL STARS

Britain's top swimmers compete in race meetings in Britain and around the world. They race in a 50-metre-long pool.

There are races for different swimming strokes. The fastest stroke is the freestyle, also called the front crawl.

Olympic gold medallist, Rebecca Adlington, swims freestyle at the British Championship.

DIVE!

Britain's divers have won Olympic medals, too. They dive from a 10-metre-high board. They must keep their body in the right position all the way down.

Tom Daley became a world champion diver when he was only 15.

DOING IT ALL

The triathlon is a very difficult event. Athletes must swim, cycle, then run, one after the other.

The Brownlee brothers, Alistair and Jonny, both won Olympic medals in the triathlon in 2012.

WINTER FUN

We don't get much snow in the UK, but we still love to do winter sports!

IN THE SNOW

Now that we can make snow and ice with machines, there are many places to ski and snowboard in Britain.

In 2014, snowboarder Jennie Jones won Britain's first ever Olympic medal in a snow sport.

Jennie Jones didn't learn to ski until she was 17. When she took up snowboarding, she became a world-beater.

ON THE ICE

The skeleton bob is one of Britain's most successful Winter Olympic sports. Competitors slide headfirst down an ice track on a tray. They reach speeds up to 128 kilometres per hour.

Skeleton bob champion Lizzie Yarnold won Olympic gold in 2014.

Curling and figure skating are both medal-winning ice sports for Britain, too.

CRAZY SPORTS

Britain is home to some crazy world sports championships. Here are three that anyone can try.

SMASH THAT NUT

Every October you can compete in the World Conker Championship in Ashton, near Northampton.

The champion must win matches by smashing the conkers of other players.

The winner is led to a conker throne and is crowned with conkers.

OUCH! I WIN!

Go to the Cotswolds to become the World Shin-Kicking Champion. You win by kicking the other players until they fall over.

The players' trousers are stuffed with straw to protect their shins.

SWIM TO VICTORY

Every year, swimmers compete in the World Bog Snorkelling Championship in Wales. They must swim through a long, muddy trench without using their arms. The winner is the swimmer with the fastest time.

Some bog swimmers make it even more difficult by wearing fancy dress.

EXTREME SPORTS

Extreme sports are exciting, but sometimes very dangerous. They involve speed, strength, daring — and often expensive gear!

EXTREME FLYING

The world's best pilots compete in the Red Bull Air Race. They fly between massive pylons to complete a course in the fastest time.

Air racing is the world's fastest motorsport. The planes reach speeds of up to 444 kilometres per hour.

The pylons in the Red Bull Air Race are 25 metres high and just 10 to 15 metres apart.

RIDING THE WAVES

Kite surfers speed across the waves on a board, pulled by an enormous kite. The wind can catch their kite and take them flying up into the air.

The best kite surfers do tricks such as grabbing their board in mid-air.

JUMP!

Skydivers jump out of an aeroplane at 1,200 to 4,000 metres. They free-fall for a while, then open their parachutes to land.

Skydivers can join hands to make shapes in the air as they hurtle down.

QUIZ

How much do you know about British sport? Test yourself with this quiz! The answers are on page 32.

1. Which sport is played at Lords?

2. Which sport is played at Wimbledon?

3. Can you name one of the riding events in three-day eventing?

4. Which sport is Lizzie Armitstead famous for?

5. Where is the British Formula One Grand Prix race held?

6. What kind of race is the Fastnet Race?

7. Lizzie Yarnold won a gold medal at the Winter Olympics. Did she win it for the skeleton bob or for curling?

GLOSSARY

division – a group of sports teams that play against each other for a championship.

dressage – a horse-riding event. The horse must do a routine of moves to win points.

freestyle – a swimming stroke, also called the front crawl.

league – a large, organised group of teams that compete against each other.

sponsored – when someone is given money for achieving something. Marathon runners are often sponsored and give the money to charity.

steeplechasing – a type of horse racing where the horses and riders jump over fences.

test match – a sports match between teams representing their country.

triathlon – a sport where there are swimming, cycling and running rounds.

velodrome – an indoor cycle track.

ANSWERS

1. Cricket is played at Lords.

2. Tennis is played at Wimbledon.

3. Dressage, show jumping and cross country are all events in three-day eventing.

4. Lizzie Armitstead is famous for cycling.

5. The British Formula One Grand Prix is held at Silverstone.

6. The Fastnet race is a yacht race.

7. Lizzie Yarnold won a gold medal for the skeleton bob.